WALKING ON SNOW

WALKING ON SNOW

Mary Guckian

Swan Press

Swan Press
32 Joy Street
Dublin 4

Copyright © with author, 2010

ISBN 978 0 956049643

Photographs by Mary Guckian

Printed by: Precision Print, Cornelscourt, Dublin 18

Dedicated to my mother, Pauline (1918-2007). She lived a long healthy and hardworking life baking bread almost every day up to three years before she passed on. Always busy with work around the farm, and knitting and sewing, in her eighties she developed a new hobby of painting on linen. Pieces of her work are treasured by friends and relations as far away as Connecticut and Florida.

Acknowledgements are due to the editors of the following literary magazines and anthologies where most of these poems appeared.

Arts Newsletter Leitrim County Council, *Awen, Beatlick, Boyne Berries, Corran Herald, Cerberus, Coffeehouse, Connections, Cutting Edge, Earthlove, Extended Wings 4, 5, Free Expression, Humanism Ireland, Ireland's Issues, Interpreters House, Irish American Post, Labour of Love, Linkway, Leitrim Guardian, Leitrim Observer, Living It, Metverse Muse, Modern Woman, News Four, New Link, Poetry Monthly, Peer Poetry, Purpose, Poiesis Number Three, Quantum Leap,* RI*POSTE, Reflections, Roscommon Champion, St. Joseph's Magazine, Sligo Champion, Studies, Weyfarers, Wildside, ZZZ Zyne, Xpose* Galway.

Seeing the Wood and the Trees, eds. Rosemarie Rowley and John Haughton

Acknowledgements are due also to the following websites where poems have been on view: Acorn, Art Arena, Kritya, Other Voices International Project.

Walking on Snow was voted the most popular poem in RI*POSTE* in 2007. Some of the poems have been placed in competitions, including Poetry on the Wall, Tallaght Libraries and Scottish Open International Poetry Competition.

I would like to thank Rathmines Writers for their support, especially James Conway, Eithne Cavanagh for editorial advice, Christine Broe and Maura O'Grady for being good friends as well as supporters over the years and to remember the late Warren O'Connell, a founder of the Workshop who was a constant and positive influence over the years, also Gwen Bond founder of *Siar Sceal*.

Contents	Page
White Frost	13
Our Round Bush	14
May Eve	15
Pulling the Curtains	16
Washboard	17
Swallows	18
Corpus Christi Procession	19
Ancient Cure	21
Family Photograph	22
J.J.	23
Fuchsia	25
Brigid	26
Walking on Snow	29
Pongers	30
Cranes and Crosses	31
Clyde Road	32
Bright Day	33
Chestnut Trees	34
Silver Birch	35
Seagulls on the Liffey Boardwalk	36
Birdsong in Joy Street	37
Registry Office	38

Contents	Page
Passing Sun	39
Leaking Tap	40
Chinese Chef with Seagulls	41
Canal Walk	42
Cold December Day	43
Red Nasturtium	44
Hammering Sounds	45
Bluestone Christmas Lights	47
Anglers at Dromod	50
The Miners' Way	51
Storm	52
Floodplains	53
Thunder	54
Castle Walls	55
Stony Path	56
Human Spirit	57
Feet Free	58
Zen Spring	59

Snow at Kiltoghert, Co. Leitrim

White Frost

White frost marks
divisions of fields
and gardens of Cloncolry.
Overgrown hedges, thorny,
transform into pillows
of ragged cotton
and tall trees dressed
in shimmering silk
quietly glow.

Stiff rushes
crunch underfoot
where robins appear
waiting for crumbs
to fall on hardened soil.
By midday, bright sun
thaws landscape
into Winter greyness.

Our Round Bush

A pink perm of luscious
hawthorn blossoms sprouted
from our round bush every year,
the bottom layer cut tightly
into a saucer shaped hedge.
Here we aired mattresses,
battering them with heavy sticks,
watched dust collapse
from red horse-hair stuffing.

Heavy woollen jumpers were
laid out to dry over the sharp
surface and thorns prodded our
fingers when we took damp
garments into the kitchen.
Hens and chickens raced
through turf-mouldy soil.
A crown of red combs
rose from turkeys' heads,
feathers opened into balloons
as they scowled in circles.

As the round bush grew taller
it sheltered saved turf
in the open shed
from hailstone showers
and falls of snow.

May Eve

On May Eve we picked
yellow flowers
from the road meadow
where a narrow stream flooded
over the ground, leaving
stems fat and rubbery.

We reverently placed
the green bunches
by doorsteps of our homes
and farm outhouses.

Making a wish for good
weather, our prayers were
for a plentiful harvest
along with abundant
fodder for our cattle.

Lively May winds
scattered the fading
petals across the farm,
heavy showers beating
them back into the earth.

Pulling the Curtains
(In memory of my Mother)

At six a.m. blackbirds with yellow nibs
peck for grubs, willie-wagtails arrow the sky
thrushes hop along trimmed hedges.
Bracing air wakes me
for the journey to Sligo hospital.

I leave the lane, drive towards the bridge.
At the bottom of Sang Hill
woodpigeons have trouble rising,
worms shrivel along the ground.

I bring three freshly ironed nightdresses.
Mammy is ready for theatre, a bit dozy,
she is wheeled off by a jolly man.
Day and night staff in pastel colours
change over, calm in their movement
from patient to patient.

Doctors come and go.
Curtains close around each bed
pain is eased,
air is filtered with disinfectant.

I walk around Sligo and pray
my mother will survive.
Television scenes full of blood
and operating theatres flood my mind.
Bookshops are a diversion
until at last I hear all is well.

Washboard

A wooden tub
full of lather is balanced
on two wooden chairs.

Knuckles hurt
from constant scrubbing
on the washboard
to take farm sweat
off cotton shirts
and striped towels.

Sheets and pillow cases
dipped in Robin Starch
rinsed in Reckitt's Blue
await drying and a hot iron.

Swallows

After years of hatching
in the same speckled bowl
that clung to the rafters of the iron roof,
long tailed swallows glided
onto our street in Spring.

A makeover, using clean wisps of hay
they prepared their Irish home
and for the next two months
we waited for babies to appear.

We watched pink mouths
work like pincers as they devoured
food from their parents
who moved in and out all day,
beaks full of grubs and worms,
their wings skimming our heads.

Soon the young take their first
flying lessons from wood planks
in preparation for the long trip to
South Africa – a four month journey -
travelling fifty miles a day.

Every year we waited anxiously
for their springtime return
delighted as they glided
back to our barn.

Corpus Christi Procession

On the night before
the annual procession
we ironed our pale blue
Child of Mary cloaks
and carefully folded
delicate lace veils,
into neat parcels.
Next morning we awoke
excited about taking part.
Parcels in the carriers,
we cycled pot-holed roads
praying the tyres would survive
over rough stones.
Wearing our Child of Mary
medals, we attended last mass
at St. Mary's Church.
Along the footpaths
people gathered, waiting
to be placed in lines
while we donned
cloaks and veils.
Male helpers wearing
right hand arm bands
arranged us in bunches
behind a row of priests
in long garments,
heavy embroidery
glistening in the sun.
Four pall bearers
carried a cloth
covered in braid ringlets
attached to four long poles

high over the priest
to shelter
the golden monstrance.
If showers came,
large umbrellas were held
by the tallest men,
and the choir sang hymns
to get us marching
in slow motion
as we prayed out loud,
veils blowing in the breeze.
We admired altars
with large vases
of lavender lilac,
red peony roses.
Honeycombs of lupins,
purple and yellow,
around the Infant of Prague
decorated shop windows.
Our Lady wore a blue veil.
Pictures of St Joseph
and the pierced heart
of the Sacred Heart filled
newly painted doorways.
Saying our prayers
with enthusiasm
we circled the town,
bought ice-cream wafers
and struggled back to reality,
facing the journey
back to the farm where many jobs
waited to be completed.

Ancient Cure

Snails nestling in cabbage heads -
we picked them
and placed the soft bodies
over warts on our hands.

They wizened on hawthorn branches
while we waited for the shrivelling
of cracked bumps
on our over-worked fingers.

Family Photograph

In her eighties
body shortened, stooped,
this frail old woman
has survived a stroke.
Her six foot son,
once a baby in her arms
now a father,
takes her by the hand.

Two rows of pearls sheen
on her navy blouse
while quietly
her granddaughter clicks,
capturing a moment
before the final lunch
of a mother
with her family.

J.J.

With *good luck to ye*
your welcome was warm,
the first to meet us
on the narrow road
to our mobile in the fields.
Barrels full of water
rattled as you drove
your tractor up and down
the road, with bales of hay
for your quiet cattle.

Your dog hopping along,
you were good friends,
his bark oozing contentment
in this boggy landscape.
Only natural he stayed nearby
when you collapsed,
watching until a neighbour
heard the tractor humming,
found you lying on damp grass.

You left in time, your road
is now a detour.
Trees are felled, diggers
push away clay and debris.
Archaeologists search
for signs of other centuries.
Busily, they rip the earth,
ruins of a water mill appear.

Your fields mourn silently
as cattle taken to the mart
are sold, hedges overgrown.
Rusty dockweed clutters
open spaces, rushes thrive.
Outside, cars stall or reverse
on this well worn road
made for horse and donkey carts.

Fuchsia

Today, red bluebells hang
from the mossy edge
of a steep ditch facing
the iron graveyard gate.
Above here is the bull field
where Sonny walked his well-fed
animal from cowshed to green grass
while funerals passed through
the gates of Kiltoghert Graveyard.
Lowing sounds, a backdrop
to sad silence of each body
entering the newly dug cold clay.

Brigid

After her two bachelor
brothers died, Brigid
lived on her own,
feeding hens, milking cows,
cooking daily meals.
She enjoyed listening
to the radio, hearing the news
about other towns, other cities,
other countries, and
the weather forecast.

Walking around her small farm
a round tam cap
lightly covering her head,
she lived quietly,
close to the land, never
a cross word from her lips,
she never gossiped, borrowed
or stole, lived contentedly
in her home.

Five people at her funeral
her passing not worth
a mention, no politicians
no votes, no show-offs here
rushing to be seen.

Yet it makes no difference,
we all end up in the same
grey earth and cold clay,
no matter how we live
our lives or make ends meet.

Old Road near Dromod, Co. Leitrim

Walking on Snow

On freshly fallen
snowflakes,
layers of delicate
petals fragment
beneath my feet –
the delicacy of nature
fragile as relationships
crumbling in the
wee small hours
of another night.

Pongers

Drifting into sleep
I hear beer cans rattle
outside windows
of my terraced house.
No green space here
to absorb sound.
In the wind they blow
with a clattering bang.

Dozing, I see pongers
recycled from tin cans
by the travellers,
and filled with milk
for young calves.

Those busy craftsmen
smoothed edges
of shiny tin
making the pongers safe.
They bartered them
for milk, fresh vegetables.

Cranes and Crosses

It is St. Brigid's Eve
and eleven long armed cranes
hang from fragile clouds over
our cosy homes in Ringsend.
Above the empty Gasometer
men caged in cranes all day
are suspended between earth and sky.

They have guided clumpy loads
to transform an empty site
into colossal living spaces
of tightly packed containers
now homes for single people
and smart Google operators
who puff on cigarettes outside
in the cool frosty air.

The interweaving of stark metal
above my head takes me back
to the last century and away
from chill of cement and glass.

I walk again on purl-stitched soil,
patterned by cattle footprints
where we pulled green stalks
from damp earth, sucked the dry
coconut flavour from inside
green stems, savoured the tang.
With a scissors we cut bundles
of tall rushes to weave
frail crosses which we placed
over altars in our homes
for St. Brigid's Day.

Clyde Road

Tall laburnums
with ringlets
create a canopy
over pedestrians
on Clyde Road.
When cars disturb
this monastic space
a shower of seeds
parachute over
the concrete
leaving a lemon
carpet cushioning
the morning traffic.

Bright Day

(In memory of Warren O'Connell)

Eightieth birthday party,
and April colours spurt
from corners of gardens.
Hedges hide movement
of birds building nests.
Leaving our heavy coats
at home, we are embraced
by warm air and celebrate
as the slow wizening
of another winter
bursts into song.

Chestnut Trees

Secure and stately chestnut trees
fill our front windows with pink
candelabra on a May morning.
The candyfloss blossoms give
light to this grim area
of bedsits, small flats.

These trees have witnessed
much change, yet they continue
to flood from their branches
brilliant blushing petals,
bringing a delicate grace
to an old Edwardian street.

Silver Birch

Silver birch trees billow
their drindl skirts, gusts of wind
shake layers of green flounces.
Blustering air shudders my body into life.

Struggling with the computer, I ease
my thoughts into ordering books
on recycled paper for the library stock.

During the day, silver skin glows
on firm trunks, sun brightens space.
Under heavy green cloaks branches
thicken year after year, adorning
empty space outside Victorian windows.

Seagulls on the Liffey Boardwalk

White-breasted seagulls
form an army of drummers
on the painted handrails
of the Liffey boardwalk.
They gaze around, then fly off,
leaving a graffiti
of guano on shining wood.

I step on to solid footing
away from traffic blare.
Sturdy railings save
children from tottering
into dark pulsating water.
Ethnic groups bring glamour
as they eat snacks, drink coffee
roll cigarettes, lick ice cream.

The River Liffey's odour
tangles with perfume gushing
from purple and pink begonias.
Fuchsia bells dance gently
for backpackers who read books,
study maps, write diaries.

Seated close to the water
rowers paddle lanky oars.
They pull in rhythm
with the coxwain's orders
bursting through the loud hailer.
Oarsmen stay in tune
with the great river
as it slides towards the Irish sea.

Birdsong in Joy Street

On a bright June evening
birds sing in Joy Street,
sweet sounds mingle with noisy
clampers – yellow shovels lock
the front wheels of cars.

Air is clean after a heavy downpour
shoppers rush towards Eurospar
before closing time, meet
young mothers pushing prams
around the park at Dock Street.

This is the place where birds hide,
build nests, rear chicks
and fill Joy Street with birdsong.

Registry Office

I see plants springing new life
in my window-box today
and wild honeysuckle grows
from strength to strength.

Walking along Grand Canal Street
I see couples preparing to take risks,
bind their lives with signatures
at the Registry office.

Passing Sun

Passing sun blinds my eyes
shingle rattles under my feet,
a hairy dog snaps at my heels.
Proud parents struggle to push
prams through damp sand.

Young boys fly a lone kite
under delicate blue skies
caressed by white steam puffing
from red and white chimneys
of Poolbeg power station.

On level grey cement
arthritic people exercise
after hip operations – crutches
and Zimmer frames for support
while they adjust to plastic parts
now helping aged bodies
to enjoy new life.

Leaking Tap

Monotonous sounds
clutter my room
as drop after drop
from a leaking tap
chants all night.
Thinking of morning,
and of having to face
a long day, I force
myself to cope
my head fuzzy
my body drained.

Chinese Chef with Seagulls

A Chinese chef feeds seagulls
down on the Dublin docks.
White feathered, they fly over
the River Liffey, dive for crumbs
as the man flings left-over food
from a bowl he has carried out
of an Italian restaurant on Lime Street.

Like a bunch of friends
at a midday party
they screech and scowl,
amusing the foreign chef
who surfaces for air to escape
a sweltering kitchen.

Gracefully the gulls take off,
beaks loaded, their calls crackle
above cranes and diggers.

Canal Walk

I love to walk
by the Grand Canal
in the morning,
a path of gold crackling
beneath my feet.
I slowly come to life,
and absorb rippling
sounds of water
while reeds tingle
in the gentle breeze.

Brisk air prepares me
for a long tedious
day behind a desk
typing and filing,
answering the phone,
keeping customers happy,
demanding bosses content.

Cold December Day

Damp air hangs
over Pearse Street
on a cold December day.
Along the footpath
oily steel blue bulbs
with a frosty sheen
blink from windows.

Traffic lights turn
red for seconds.
The temperature rises,
green lights return,
punch the muggy air,
bring colour back
to a leafless street.

At South Dock Square
red matchstick poles
reflect on icy water
of the Grand Canal.
Weaving waves
forge movement –
a reminder of logs
blazing on hearth stones
at Winter time.

Red Nasturtium

A lone red
nasturtium
glows starlike
this Christmas Day.
It trails over
the wild Woodbine
in my patio.
Its light shines
through greyness,
keeping a hint
of Summer alive.

Hammering Sounds

Hammering sounds
from Barrow Street
hang around my home
in the morning
as metal hits metal
and the Metro Verde
building rises
to sixteen storeys.

I take milk from the fridge
and remember carts
packed with creamery cans,
horses and donkeys
swaying side to side
climbing Mary Ann's Hill.

Echoes of iron
ring across the farm
as cans are pushed
across the platform
of Kiltoghert Creamery,
emptied into vats
for buttermaking,
then shifted back on shiny
dark stone and refilled
with skim milk.

When my father
was in hospital
I waited at the lane
for a farmer
to carry our milk
to the creamery.
Despite packed carts
to my childish delight,
one kind person
always lifted a full can
on to his daily load.

Bluestone Christmas Lights

Bluestone spray coloured lights
decorate the tall Christmas tree
that crowns Grafton Street,
sharp shapes piercing the night sky.

On foggy evenings shoppers
scurry in all directions, loaded
with parcels and designer bags
they prepare for celebrations.

The cold colour triggers pictures
of my father spraying lanky leaves
in potato ridges and watching blue
showers cover young stalks.

Under soil, baby potatoes endured
frosty nights, Autumn digging
produced a year's abundance of food.

The atmosphere around takes me back
to dinners full of floury flavours
while I try to concentrate on shopping
for my annual Christmas presents.

Nasturtiums on the barn window

Anglers at Dromod

Anglers sit all day
gazing into dark water.
In front of them, thin
nylon lines gently flop
on the cold river where
they wait for fish to bite.

Hours pass before rods
are hauled from dark depths
of heaving water, colour
changing as blood flows
where embedded hooks distort
the jaws of shiny fish.

After weighing, the net
is emptied and fish swim back
into the river with broken wounds.
Hidden among the reeds
fishermen wearing green wax coats
blend into the landscape.

The Miners' Way

High at Arigna Mines
the day is grey.
Here to visit, I ponder
on generations of miners.

In dark passages
they lay on their sides enduring
constant drip as they scraped
a living from the damp shale.

In the Visitors' Centre
photos tell of men, blackened,
their breathing damaged
from dust-choked lungs
- their lives shortened.

Storm

Restless trees shiver,
bend with the raging storm
as frenzied movement cracks branches
and torrents of curled leaves
carpet the damp ground.

News on television shows
destruction of monumental trees
crashing on top of cars
and crushing animals running
for shelter from the sudden storm.

Floodplains

Rain deluges
from celestial clouds –
rivers flow, lakes form
in low lying land
where cattle drink
from the soft edge
of green banks.

Small farmers like my father
cleared bracken from streams
on dark days, ensuring
free flow of clean water.

Without constant tending
veins of the earth
become blocked
breaking the steady
movement of currents.

Over years, thriving growth
chokes narrow rivulets
flooding new places.

Thunder

Mist moves across fields
and flowers shiver,
petals turn inwards
reaching back to buds hiding
from thunder that shakes
buildings around this place.
I feel torn apart, but then
the sun shines, new strength
comes from strange sources.
Seeds take root, trees grow
to great heights, making me
wonder how I ever doubted
this force, this everlasting
force that moves me on and on.

Castle Walls

In the grounds
around the castle
I see each century
shaped in the history
of this worn building.

Built for lords
and ladies in times
of cheap labour.
In our own era
the walls echoed
with the sound of prayers
and psalms of nuns.

Now a hotel,
people pay to relax
and hone their lives
amid stained glass
and sturdy stone walls.

Stony Path

As I walk on the stony path
light shines from a cloudless sky,
coloured shards of broken glass
crushed between stones
dazzle my eyes
in the shimmering sun.

Moving towards the big house,
windowless and empty,
I trample on memories -
once wine flowed into goblets
arranged on long tables
to greet men returning laden
with wildlife from forest shoots.

Strips of light burst from leafy frills
shaking and dancing
above my throbbing head,
perfumed clean air gives back
energy to my tired feet
as I plod along the stony path.

Human Spirit

Each calamity a nation suffers
brings tragedy and despair.
As bombs fall, planes crash
cataclysmic moments are written
into our history books.

Broken bodies are buried,
families left behind are fragile.
Through the voices of children
new lives are forged
and we begin again.

The weight of confusion
on every generation causes tension
and panic - yet with camaraderie
we can face our differences,
our pinched prejudices, move forward.
The human spirit never dies.

Feet Free

Addicted to spongy earth
I walk in bare feet
where cool grass
massages thirsty skin.

My clogged head sheds
peelings - leftovers gathered
from the daily grind
of winter months.

Shoeless, I lie in cut meadow
listening to the rattling herbs
dried out with summer sun.

Zen Spring

Dandelions
yellow dots on fields
in April

With a shovel
you dig into dark soil
I fill it with plants

Swallows take a rest
on electric wires
after a shower

Drips of water
hang from branches
pearls fall

Cherry blossoms
on Dublin City quays
welcome visitors

Greenfly covers
healthy nasturtium leaves
in the window box

Across the road
birds take flight
from chimney pots

Lanky daffodils
in the Leitrim ditches
give way to Spring

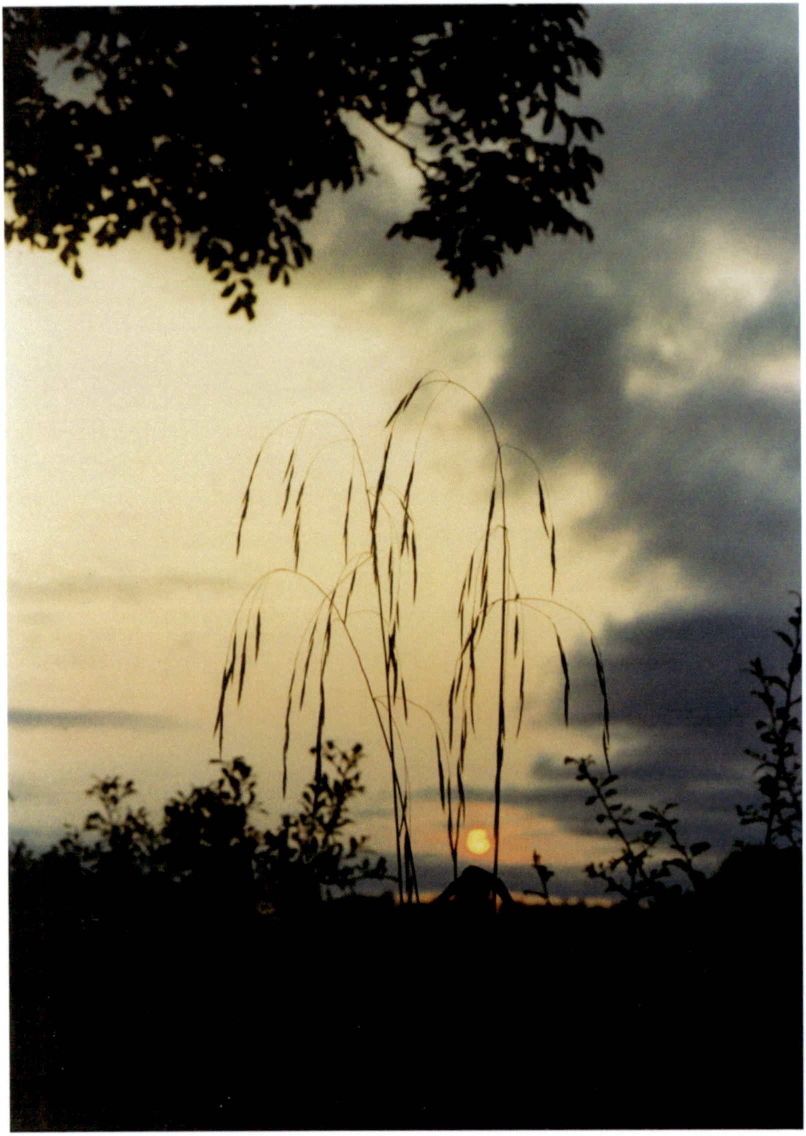